Poets From The West Midlands

Edited By Wendy Laws

First published in Great Britain in 2019 by:

Young Writers
Remus House
Coltsfoot Drive
Peterborough
PE2 9BF
Telephone: 01733 890066
Website: www.youngwriters.co.uk

All Rights Reserved
Book Design by Ashley Janson
© Copyright Contributors 2019
SB ISBN 978-1-78988-418-0
Printed and bound in the UK by BookPrintingUK
Website: www.bookprintinguk.com
YB0401CZ

FOREWORD

Dear Reader,

Are you ready to get your thinking caps on to puzzle your way through this wonderful collection?

Young Writers are proud to introduce our new poetry competition, *My First Riddle*, designed to introduce Reception pupils to the delights of poetry. Riddles are a great way to introduce children to the use of poetic expression, including description, similes and expanded noun phrases, as well as encouraging them to 'think outside the box' by providing clues without giving the answer away immediately. Some pupils were given a series of riddle templates to choose from, giving them a framework within which to shape their ideas.

Their answers could be whatever or whoever their imaginations desired; from people to places, animals to objects, food to seasons. All of us here at Young Writers believe in the importance of inspiring young children to produce creative writing, including poetry, and we feel that seeing their own riddles in print will ignite that spark of creativity.

We hope you enjoy riddling your way through this book as much as we enjoyed reading all the entries.

CONTENTS

Independent Entries

Dax Nicholds (4)   1

Berkswich CE (C) Primary School, Walton

Phoebe Holmes (4)	2
Lacey Andrews (4)	3
Daniel Orlando Henriques (4)	4
Ilythea Godbeer (4)	5
Evan Lamond (5)	6
Noah Marc Fitzsimmons (5)	7
Otto Tedstone (4)	8
James Mason (4)	9
Isaac Fisher (4)	10
Fraser Gabriel (4)	11
Kiera Binns (4)	12
Isla Taylor-Farshbaf (4)	13
Hugh Cartlidge (4)	14
Rosalie Smith (5)	15
Wilfred Bhageerutty (5)	16
Finley Broomhall (4)	17

Binley Woods Primary School, Binley Woods

Alfie George Hopkinson (5)	18
Aman Dhesi (5)	19
Georgia Cooper (4)	20
Sophie Jadesola Onilari (5)	21
Connie Strickland (4)	22
Oliver Jones (4)	23
Rakeem Noor (4)	24

Birds Bush Primary School, Belgrave

Isabelle Thompson (5)	25
Caitlyn Jade Taylor (4)	26
Poppy Tarrant (5)	27
Lacey Gilbert (5)	28
Ruben Caveney (5)	29
Casey-Rae Prees (4)	30
Dylan Bache (4)	31
Eva Rose Nerney (4)	32
Charlie King (5)	33
Olivia Leatherland (4)	34
Archie King (5)	35
Lucy-May Hall (4)	36
Elleigh Green-Buckley (4)	37

Bishopton Primary School, Stratford-Upon-Avon

Logan Hague (5), Daisy, Chloe & Szymon	38
Oliver Brown (4)	39
Alfie Cox (4)	40

Fulford Primary School, Fulford

Scarlett Baughen (5)	41
Aurora Ava Copeland (5)	42
Daniel Philip Goold (4)	43
Louis Boulton (5)	44
Molly Ashworth (5)	45
Max Bishop (5)	46
Fergus Ruaridh Gill (5)	47

Harper Bell SDA School, Birmingham

Semi Awoniranye (5)	48
Marcel Baker (5)	49
Ashantae Samuel (4)	50
Ruel Worrell (4)	51
Jada Johnson (5)	52
Fatima Jallow (5)	53
Nasir (4)	54
Esther Nealson (5)	55
Ayanna Mambrini (4)	56
Tasia Berryman (4)	57

Haughton St Giles Primary Academy, Haughton

Isaac Richards (5)	58
Lily Duffett (5)	59
Amy Seville (5)	60
Axel Molinier (5)	61

Highfields Primary School, Rowley Regis

Charlie Elwell (4)	62
Jennifer Laura Floyd (4)	63
Lola Payton (4)	64

Holywell Primary & Nursery School, Rubery

Isabelle Davey (5)	65
Jonah Clancy (5)	66
Naomi Gabriella Anne Young (5)	67
Emilia Lynott (5)	68
Piper Perkins (5)	69
Lewis Clarke (4)	70
Gracie Medler (4)	71
Noah Holder (5)	72
Evie Clarke (4)	73
Oliver James Perry (4)	74

Martin Wilson School, Castlefields

Anneliese Cooper (4)	75
Libby Hall (5)	76
William Woolf-Farr (5)	77
Ling To (4)	78
Florence Cheadle (5)	79
Khaled Al Mohammad (4)	80
Maria Maunder (4)	81
Bella-Rose Bowen (4)	82
Sonny Ray Gibbons (5)	83
Aiden Morris (5)	84
Layla Haddock (5)	85
Luna Morris (5)	86

Moor Green Primary Academy, Moseley

Indiana Starr (4)	87
Freya Lewis-Jackson (4)	88
Laiba Aslam (4)	89
Zahra Assad Dar (4)	90
Mabel Orbach (5)	91
Max De Jong (4)	92
Florence Orbach (5)	93
Rory Tyldesley Hosfield (5)	94
Ava Roberts (5)	95
Aria van Leeuwen (5)	96
Finlay Joe Biles (5)	97
Amara Aisha Ali (4)	98
Zahra Hinds (5)	99
Amelia Suliman (4)	100
Mariah McEwan (4)	101

Oswestry School, Oswestry

Olivia Potts (4)	102
Florence Everly Ruscoe (4)	103
Edward Barker (4)	104
Ella Osselton (4)	105
Eleonora Rekikoski (5)	106
Curran Dhawan (4)	107

Rugby Free Primary School, Rugby

Roman Lane (5)	108
Sophia Donnell (5)	109
Poppy Wood (4)	110
Ruben Dijkstra (4)	111
Mia Lily Whittingham (4)	112
Anne Dewes (4)	113
Isaac Love (5)	114
Eliza Houghton (4)	115
Theoren Wilson (4)	116
Teddy James (4)	117
Khadeejah Iftekhar (4)	118

Squirrel Hayes First School, Biddulph

Connor Wilshaw (5), Lillie Beckett (5) & Brooke	119
Maximus Hirst Malbon (5), Thomas & Shonalisa	120
Liam Rutter (5), Aiden Greensmith (5) & Oscar Till (5)	121

St Anne's Catholic Primary School, Birmingham

Ryan Rushid (5) & Sumayyah	122
Azeem Majid (5)	123
Eleesa Manaa (5)	124
Alice Boaretto Stuelp (4)	125

St Benedict's RC Primary Academy, Atherstone

Michael Gregory (5)	126
Emily Rose Owen (4)	127
Henry Scott (4)	128
Jessica Scott (4)	129
Sienna Elsie Stone (4)	130
Alexander Theocharous (4)	131
Natasha Vanessa Radziwonka (4)	132
Jeffrey Smith (5)	133

Isabella Mobley (4)	134
Milosz Gaciag (5)	135
Daisy Taylor (5)	136
Bobby Hill (5)	137
Apheia Thompson (5)	138

St Thomas' CE (A) Primary School, Kidsgrove

Daniel George Machin (5)	139
Annabelle Massey (4) & Carter Smyk (5)	140
William Dolman (5) & Lewis	141
Millie Brown (4)	142
George Halstead (4)	143
Esmae Murfitt (5)	144
Charlie Sambrooks (5) & Rhys Simcock (5)	145
Elliott Churchill (5)	146
Rowan Bennett (4)	147
Sammy Tunnicliffe (5)	148
Aimee Rose Kathryn Phillips (4)	149
Kai Murphy (5)	150
Layla Beckensall (5)	151
Lexi Rose Bloor (5)	152
Joshua Dillion (4)	153

Stoke Minster CE Primary Academy, Stoke-On-Trent

Jake Sloane-Bulger (4)	154
Victoria Tivesi Gondwe (4)	155
Dakota-Marie Cole (5)	156
Erin Adams (5) & Skye	157
Frankie Bishop (4)	158
Amadeus Wilson (4) & Jemimah	159
Abdul Hannan (4)	160
Hiba Inayat (4)	161
Aailyah Jefferies (5)	162
Mohammad Musa Tanveer (5)	163

Stratford Preparatory School, Stratford-Upon-Avon

Isabella Johanna Koch (5)	164
Florence Skelton (5)	165
Elizabeth Robotham (5)	166
Alice-Rose Domoney (4)	167
Harriet Griffiths (4)	168
Rory Withers (4)	169

Timberley Academy, Birmingham

Levi Dunn (5)	170
Poppy Marie Nicholls (5)	171
Rayyan Aiheve (4)	172
Ellie-Mai Draisey (4)	173
Jayden Lees (5)	174
Carlisle Anatole (4)	175
Megan Hennessy (4)	176
Rueben-Lee Pickett (4)	177
Hannah Haji (4)	178
Kai Teece (5)	179
Kaitlyn Collins (4)	180
Tommy Ray Hopton (5)	181
Joshua John Edwards (5)	182
Zachary Sheldon (5)	183
Ray Jackson Maxwell (5)	184
Amarn Imran (4)	185
Maya Douglas (4)	186
Lexie-Louise Rice (5)	187
Evan Ridsdill (5)	188
Vinnie Griffiths (4)	189
Casey-Rose Dutton-Jones (4)	190
Teah-Nevaeh Queely (5)	191
Violet Dunne (5)	192
Blake Powers (4)	193
Lewis Daniel Read (4)	194
Alicia Rebecca McAdorey (4)	195
Lailah-Rose Harris (4)	196
Isla Wilson (5)	197

Weston Infant Academy, Weston Coyney

Paisley Rae Birks (5)	198
Rosie Reid (5), Jacob & Chloe Hilton (4)	199
Olivia Ritchie (4)	200
Jack Edward Sidley (4), Millie-May Walklate (5), Caitlin Louise Sherratt (4) & Aayla	201
Rosalie Weston (5)	202
Evie Lawton (5) & Lana Williams (4)	203
Lacey May Shaw (5)	204
Isabela Grace Davis (5)	205
Scarlett Rose Kudlek (5)	206
Eliana Sagoa (5)	207
Amelia-Grace Dunn (4)	208
Edward Leslie (5)	209
Freddie Adamson (4)	210
Ruby-Jo Clewes (5)	211
Kacie-Jane Slater (4)	212
Charlie Milne (4)	213
Jesse James Fox (4)	214
Eva Barber (4)	215
George Pinto (5) & Eliza-Jayne	216
Sophie Rose Mundy (5)	217
Macie Banks (4), Jacob, Archie Mark Eastlake (4), Jack & Jaden	218
Jacoby Blackaby (4) & Alesha Burley (4)	219
Guinevere Bennett (4)	220
Lilly Banks (4)	221
Harvey Mantle (4)	222
Cobie Thomas Emery (5)	223

Yardley Primary School, Birmingham

Inaya Choudhury-Rana (5)	224
Noor-Alaynah Usman (4)	225
Xaavier Mahmood (4)	226
Joel Mason (5)	227

THE RIDDLES

Dax's First Riddle

What could she be?
Follow the clues and see.

She looks like **a very big cat.**
She sounds like **a dinosaur, now how about that.**
She smells like **an orange, all round and juicy.**
She feels **so furry, I have named her Lucy.**
She tastes **lots and lots of bright red meat, she loves it as a nice tasty treat.**

Have you guessed what she could be?
Look below and you will see,
She is...

Answer: Lucy the tiger.

Dax Nicholds (4)

Phoebe's First Riddle

What could it be?
Follow the clues and see.

It looks like **a baby dog**.
It sounds like **woof, woof!**
It smells like **a new baby**.
It feels like **a soft teddy bear**.
It tastes like... **oh you can't eat it!**

Have you guessed what it could be?
Look below and you will see,
It is...

Answer: A puppy of course!

Phoebe Holmes (4)
Berkswich CE (C) Primary School, Walton

Lacey's First Riddle

What could it be?
Follow the clues and see.

It looks like **hard brown squares**.
It sounds like **silence**.
It smells like **heaven to me!**
It feels like **it could melt in my hands**.
It tastes like **smooth, milky cocoa**.

Have you guessed what it could be?
Look below and you will see,
It is...

Answer: Chocolate.

Lacey Andrews (4)
Berkswich CE (C) Primary School, Walton

Daniel's First Riddle

What could it be?
Follow the clues and see.

It looks like **a yummy square**.
It sounds like **a crackling eggshell**.
It smells like **cream**.
It feels **smooth and bumpy**.
It tastes like **a mild sugar and spice**.

Have you guessed what it could be?
Look below and you will see,
It is...

Answer: A *cream cracker.*

Daniel Orlando Henriques (4)
Berkswich CE (C) Primary School, Walton

Ilythea's First Riddle

What could it be?
Follow the clues and see.

It looks like **lots of white and pink**.
It sounds like **chirping birds**.
It smells like **cut grass**.
It feels like **warm after the cold**.
It tastes like **Easter eggs, yum!**

Have you guessed what it could be?
Look below and you will see,
It is...

Answer: Spring.

Ilythea Godbeer (4)
Berkswich CE (C) Primary School, Walton

Evan's First Riddle

What could it be?
Follow the clues and see.

It looks **blue**.
It sounds like **swish, roar, crash!**
It smells like **fish and boats**.
It feels **wet and gritty**.
It tastes like **fish and chips**.

Have you guessed what it could be?
Look below and you will see,
It is...

Answer: *The sea.*

Evan Lamond (5)
Berkswich CE (C) Primary School, Walton

Noah's First Riddle

What could it be?
Follow the clues and see.

It looks like **white fluffy clouds**.
It sounds like *pop, pop!*
It smells like **sweet butter**.
It feels like **foam**.
It tastes **yummy!**

Have you guessed what it could be?
Look below and you will see,
It is...

Answer: Popcorn.

Noah Marc Fitzsimmons (5)
Berkswich CE (C) Primary School, Walton

Otto's First Riddle

What could it be?
Follow the clues and see.

It looks like **an army group**.
It sounds like **creeping**.
It smells like **sewers**.
It feels **squidgy**.
It tastes **pizza**.

Have you guessed what it could be?
Look below and you will see,
It is...

Answer: A Teenage Mutant Ninja Turtle.

Otto Tedstone (4)
Berkswich CE (C) Primary School, Walton

James' First Riddle

What could it be?
Follow the clues and see.

It looks like **a green ball**.
It sounds **crunchy**.
It smells like **leaves and grass**.
It feels like **a smooth ball**.
It tastes like **sweets**.

Have you guessed what it could be?
Look below and you will see,
It is...

Answer: An apple.

James Mason (4)
Berkswich CE (C) Primary School, Walton

Isaac's First Riddle

What could it be?
Follow the clues and see.

It looks like **jelly**.
It sounds like **nothing**.
It smells like **sweeties**.
It feels like **goo**.
It tastes like **strawberry**.

Have you guessed what it could be?
Look below and you will see,
It is...

Answer: Strawberry jam.

Isaac Fisher (4)
Berkswich CE (C) Primary School, Walton

Fraser's First Riddle

What could it be?
Follow the clues and see.

It looks like **water or solid**.
It sounds like **wibble, wobble!**
It smells like **fruit**.
It feels **squishy**.
It tastes like **sweets**.

Have you guessed what it could be?
Look below and you will see,
It is...

Answer: Jelly.

Fraser Gabriel (4)
Berkswich CE (C) Primary School, Walton

Kiera's First Riddle

What could it be?
Follow the clues and see.

It looks like **a cricket ball**.
It sounds like **'chapel'**.
It smells **fruity**.
It feels **smooth**.
It tastes **sweet**.

Have you guessed what it could be?
Look below and you will see,
It is...

Answer: An apple.

Kiera Binns (4)
Berkswich CE (C) Primary School, Walton

Isla's First Riddle

What could it be?
Follow the clues and see.

It looks like **a circle**.
It sounds **crunchy**.
It smells like **jam**.
It feels **squidgy**.
It tastes like **strawberry**.

Have you guessed what it could be?
Look below and you will see,
It is...

Answer: A doughnut.

Isla Taylor-Farshbaf (4)
Berkswich CE (C) Primary School, Walton

Hugh's First Riddle

What could it be?
Follow the clues and see.

It looks **see-through**.
It sounds **splashy**.
It smells like **nothing**.
It feels **cold**.
It tastes like **nothing**.

Have you guessed what it could be?
Look below and you will see,
It is...

Answer: Water.

Hugh Cartlidge (4)
Berkswich CE (C) Primary School, Walton

Rosalie's First Riddle

What could it be?
Follow the clues and see.

It looks **big**.
It sounds like *roar!*
It smells **old**.
It feels **smooth**.
It tastes like **a rock**.

Have you guessed what it could be?
Look below and you will see,
It is...

Answer: A dinosaur.

Rosalie Smith (5)
Berkswich CE (C) Primary School, Walton

Wilfred's First Riddle

What could it be?
Follow the clues and see.

It looks like **the sun**.
It sounds like **a melon**.
It smells **clean**.
It feels **squishy**.
It tastes **tangy**.

Have you guessed what it could be?
Look below and you will see,
It is...

Answer: A lemon.

Wilfred Bhageerutty (5)
Berkswich CE (C) Primary School, Walton

Finley's First Riddle

What could it be?
Follow the clues and see.

It looks like **glass**.
It sounds like **splashes**.
It smells **fresh**.
It feels **wet**.
It tastes like **water**.

Have you guessed what it could be?
Look below and you will see,
It is...

Answer: *Rain*.

Finley Broomhall (4)
Berkswich CE (C) Primary School, Walton

Alfie's First Riddle

What could it be?
Follow the clues and see.

It looks like **a cuddly toy with paws, ears and a black button nose.**
It sounds **crunchy when you eat it.**
It smells **sweet and yummy.**
It feels **smooth when heated.**
It tastes like **yum, yum in my tummy.**

Have you guessed what it could be?
Look below and you will see,
It is...

Answer: A cuddly chocolate teddy.

Alfie George Hopkinson (5)
Binley Woods Primary School, Binley Woods

Aman's First Riddle

What could it be?
Follow the clues and see.

It looks like **a circle and is round**.
It sounds like *whoosh* **and hooray**.
It smells like **the outdoors and green grass**.
It feels **bouncy, hard and heavy**.
It tastes like **winning and scoring a goal**.

Have you guessed what it could be?
Look below and you will see,
It is...

Answer: A football.

Aman Dhesi (5)
Binley Woods Primary School, Binley Woods

Georgia's First Riddle

What could it be?
Follow the clues and see.

It looks like **a tiny hula hoop**.
It sounds **squidgy, chomp**.
It smells like **tomato sauce**.
It feels like **it is smooth**.
It tastes like **spaghetti**.

Have you guessed what it could be?
Look below and you will see,
It is...

Answer: A Spaghetti Hoop

Georgia Cooper (4)
Binley Woods Primary School, Binley Woods

Sophie's First Riddle

What could it be?
Follow the clues and see.

It looks like **numbers and lines**.
It sounds like **ticks and tocks**.
It smells like **lovely room scents**.
It feels like **a circle with a face**.
It tastes like **dust on glass**.

Have you guessed what it could be?
Look below and you will see,
It is...

Answer: A clock.

Sophie Jadesola Onilari (4)
Binley Woods Primary School, Binley Woods

Connie's First Riddle

What could it be?
Follow the clues and see.

It looks like **a fairy**.
It sounds like **a fluttery flyer**.
It smells like **a rose**.
It feels like **feathers**.
It tastes like **chocolate**.

Have you guessed what it could be?
Look below and you will see,
It is...

Answer: A *butterfly*.

Connie Strickland (4)
Binley Woods Primary School, Binley Woods

Oliver's First Riddle

What could it be?
Follow the clues and see.

It looks like **a hand**.
It sounds like **a high five**.
It smells like **stinky cheese**.
It feels **soft**.
It tastes **hairy**.

Have you guessed what it could be?
Look below and you will see,
It is...

Answer: A glove.

Oliver Jones (4)
Binley Woods Primary School, Binley Woods

Rakeem's First Riddle

What could it be?
Follow the clues and see.

It looks like **clear lines**.
It sounds **cold**.
It smells like **water**.
It feels like **water**.
It tastes **yucky**.

Have you guessed what it could be?
Look below and you will see,
It is...

Answer: *Rain*.

Rakeem Noor (4)
Binley Woods Primary School, Binley Woods

Isabelle's First Riddle

What could it be?
Follow the clues and see.

It looks like **stripy squares**.
It sounds like **it's cracky**.
It smells like **chocolate**.
It feels **hard**.
It tastes like **milk**.

Have you guessed what it could be?
Look below and you will see,
It is...

Answer: Chocolate.

Isabelle Thompson (5)
Birds Bush Primary School, Belgrave

Caitlyn's First Riddle

What could it be?
Follow the clues and see.

It looks like **worms**.
It sounds **quiet**.
It smells like **a banana**.
It feels like **a banana**.
It tastes like **the sea**.

Have you guessed what it could be?
Look below and you will see,
It is...

Answer: Spaghetti.

Caitlyn Jade Taylor (4)
Birds Bush Primary School, Belgrave

Poppy's First Riddle

What could it be?
Follow the clues and see.

It looks like **a triangle**.
It sounds like **nothing**.
It smells like **a biscuit**.
It feels **smooth**.
It tastes **yum!**

Have you guessed what it could be?
Look below and you will see,
It is...

Answer: Chocolate.

Poppy Tarrant (5)
Birds Bush Primary School, Belgrave

Lacey's First Riddle

What could it be?
Follow the clues and see.

It looks **brown**.
It sounds like *snap!*
It smells like **strawberries**.
It feels **hard**.
It tastes **nice**.

Have you guessed what it could be?
Look below and you will see,
It is...

Answer: Chocolate.

Lacey Gilbert (5)
Birds Bush Primary School, Belgrave

Ruben's First Riddle

What could it be?
Follow the clues and see.

It looks like **a square**.
It sounds **noisy**.
It smells like **a flower**.
It feels like **a teddy**.
It tastes **nice**.

Have you guessed what it could be?
Look below and you will see,
It is…

Answer: *Chocolate.*

Ruben Caveney (5)
Birds Bush Primary School, Belgrave

Casey-Rae's First Riddle

What could it be?
Follow the clues and see.

It looks like **jam**.
It sounds like **slime**.
It smells like **jam**.
It feels like **ice**.
It tastes like **strawberries**.

Have you guessed what it could be?
Look below and you will see,
It is...

Answer: Jelly.

Casey-Rae Prees (4)
Birds Bush Primary School, Belgrave

Dylan's First Riddle

What could it be?
Follow the clues and see.

It looks like **yellow worms**.
It sounds **quiet**.
It smells like **spaghetti**.
It feels **sticky**.
It tastes **yummy**.

Have you guessed what it could be?
Look below and you will see,
It is...

Answer: Spaghetti.

Dylan Bache (4)
Birds Bush Primary School, Belgrave

Eva's First Riddle

What could it be?
Follow the clues and see.

It looks like **a diamond shape**.
It sounds like **a bang**.
It smells **sweet**.
It feels **smooth**.
It tastes **yum!**

Have you guessed what it could be?
Look below and you will see,
It is...

Answer: Chocolate.

Eva Rose Nerney (4)
Birds Bush Primary School, Belgrave

Charlie's First Riddle

What could it be?
Follow the clues and see.

It looks like **a square**.
It sounds like *crack!*
It smells **sweet**.
It feels **hard**.
It tastes **nice**.

Have you guessed what it could be?
Look below and you will see,
It is...

Answer: Chocolate.

Charlie King (5)
Birds Bush Primary School, Belgrave

Olivia's First Riddle

What could it be?
Follow the clues and see.

It looks like **a stripy square**.
It sounds **cracky!**
It smells **chocolatey**.
It feels **hard**.
It tastes **milky**.

Have you guessed what it could be?
Look below and you will see,
It is...

Answer: Chocolate.

Olivia Leatherland (4)
Birds Bush Primary School, Belgrave

Archie's First Riddle

What could it be?
Follow the clues and see.

It looks **wobbly**.
It sounds **shaky**.
It smells like **conditioner**.
It feels **cold**.
It tastes **tickly**.

Have you guessed what it could be?
Look below and you will see,
It is...

Answer: Jelly.

Archie King (5)
Birds Bush Primary School, Belgrave

Lucy-May's First Riddle

What could it be?
Follow the clues and see.

It looks **wobbly**.
It sounds **juicy**.
It smells like **strawberry**.
It feels **soft**.
It tastes **sweet**.

Have you guessed what it could be?
Look below and you will see,
It is...

Answer: Jelly.

Lucy-May Hall (4)
Birds Bush Primary School, Belgrave

Elleigh's First Riddle

What could it be?
Follow the clues and see.

It looks **wriggly**.
It sounds **jiggly**.
It smells **sweet**.
It feels **soft**.
It tastes like **sweets**.

Have you guessed what it could be?
Look below and you will see,
It is...

Answer: Jelly.

Elleigh Green-Buckley (4)
Birds Bush Primary School, Belgrave

Our First Riddle

What could it be?
Follow the clues and see.

It looks like **an orange animal with a pink nose**.
It sounds like **a loud roar**.
It smells **stinky**.
It feels like **a soft teddy bear**.
It tastes **yuck**.

Have you guessed what it could be?
Look below and you will see,
It is...

Answer: A tiger.

Logan Hague (5), Daisy, Chloe & Szymon
Bishopton Primary School, Stratford-Upon-Avon

Oliver's First Riddle

What could it be?
Follow the clues and see.

It looks like **a climbing koala**.
It sounds like **a cheeky boy**.
It smells like **stinky feet**.
It feels like **soft wool**.
It tastes like **rotten eggs**.

Have you guessed what it could be?
Look below and you will see,
It is...

Answer: A monkey.

Oliver Brown (4)
Bishopton Primary School, Stratford-Upon-Avon

Alfie's First Riddle

What could it be?
Follow the clues and see.

It looks like **a golden sun**.
It sounds like **a roar**.
It smells like **good food**.
It feels like **soft fur**.
It tastes like **sweets**.

Have you guessed what it could be?
Look below and you will see,
It is...

Answer: A lion.

Alfie Cox (4)
Bishopton Primary School, Stratford-Upon-Avon

Scarlett's First Riddle

What could it be?
Follow the clues and see.

It looks like **a nice home**.
It sounds like **birds tweeting**.
It smells like **food sizzling in a pan**.
It feels like **home**.
It tastes like **scrumptious food**.

Have you guessed what it could be?
Look below and you will see,
It is...

Answer: *Toad Hall.*

Scarlett Baughen (5)
Fulford Primary School, Fulford

Aurora's First Riddle

What could it be?
Follow the clues and see.

It looks like **a nature house**.
It sounds like **brum, brum!**
It smells like **chicken pie**.
It feels **warm and cosy**.
It tastes like **jam and toast**.

Have you guessed what it could be?
Look below and you will see,
It is…

Answer: *Toad Hall*.

Aurora Ava Copeland (5)
Fulford Primary School, Fulford

Daniel's First Riddle

What could it be?
Follow the clues and see.

It looks like **lovely flowers**.
It sounds like *ribbit, ribbit!*
It smells like **fish**.
It feels **squelchy**.
It tastes like **a fishy picnic**.

Have you guessed what it could be?
Look below and you will see,
It is...

Answer: The riverbank.

Daniel Philip Goold (4)
Fulford Primary School, Fulford

Louis' First Riddle

What could it be?
Follow the clues and see.

It looks like **squirrels**.
It sounds like **crunching leaves**.
It smells like **badgers**.
It feels like **squelchy mud**.
It tastes like **honey from bees**.

Have you guessed what it could be?
Look below and you will see,
It is...

Answer: *Wild Wood.*

Louis Boulton (5)
Fulford Primary School, Fulford

Molly's First Riddle

What could it be?
Follow the clues and see.

It looks **big and beautiful**.
It sounds like **chattering people**.
It smells like **yummy food**.
It feels like **comfy sofas**.
It tastes like **worms**.

Have you guessed what it could be?
Look below and you will see,
It is...

Answer: Toad Hall.

Molly Ashworth (5)
Fulford Primary School, Fulford

Max's First Riddle

What could it be?
Follow the clues and see.

It looks like **a scary place**.
It sounds like **howling ghosts**.
It smells like **foxes**.
It feels like **prickly holly**.
It tastes like **honey**.

Have you guessed what it could be?
Look below and you will see,
It is...

Answer: Wild Wood.

Max Bishop (5)
Fulford Primary School, Fulford

Fergus' First Riddle

What could it be?
Follow the clues and see.

It looks like **scary shadows**.
It sounds like **howling ghosts**.
It smells like **badgers**.
It feels like **hard bricks**.
It tastes like **honey**.

Have you guessed what it could be?
Look below and you will see,
It is...

Answer: *Wild Wood.*

Fergus Ruaridh Gill (5)
Fulford Primary School, Fulford

Semi's First Riddle

What could it be?
Follow the clues and see.

It looks like **lots of red**.
It sounds like **lots of noise**.
It smells like **a dumpling**.
It feels like **a celebration**.
It tastes like **good food**.

Have you guessed what it could be?
Look below and you will see,
It is...

Answer: Chinese new year.

Semi Awoniranye (5)
Harper Bell SDA School, Birmingham

Marcel's First Riddle

What could it be?
Follow the clues and see.

It looks like **feathers**.
It sounds like **flapping wings**.
It smells like **a smelly rat**.
It feels like **a soft goat**.
It tastes like **rice**.

Have you guessed what it could be?
Look below and you will see,
It is...

Answer: A rooster.

Marcel Baker (5)
Harper Bell SDA School, Birmingham

Ashantae's First Riddle

What could it be?
Follow the clues and see.

It looks like **lots of colours**.
It sounds like **a big bang**.
It smells like **fire**.
It feels like **the hot sun**.
It tastes like **popcorn**.

Have you guessed what it could be?
Look below and you will see,
It is...

Answer: *A firework.*

Ashantae Samuel (4)
Harper Bell SDA School, Birmingham

Ruel's First Riddle

What could it be?
Follow the clues and see.

It looks like **a long snake**.
It sounds like **a very loud roar**.
It smells like **hot fire**.
It feels like **spikes**.
It tastes like **smoke**.

Have you guessed what it could be?
Look below and you will see,
It is...

Answer: A dragon.

Ruel Worrell (4)
Harper Bell SDA School, Birmingham

Jada's First Riddle

What could it be?
Follow the clues and see.

It looks like **a rainbow**.
It sounds like **a loud noise**.
It smells like **burning**.
It feels like **a hot flame**.
It tastes **disgusting**.

Have you guessed what it could be?
Look below and you will see,
It is...

Answer: A firework.

Jada Johnson (5)
Harper Bell SDA School, Birmingham

Fatima's First Riddle

What could it be?
Follow the clues and see.

It looks like **lots of Cola**.
It sounds like **a big bang**.
It smells like **smoke**.
It feels like **a hot fire**.
It tastes like **smoke**.

Have you guessed what it could be?
Look below and you will see,
It is...

Answer: *A firework.*

Fatima Jallow (5)
Harper Bell SDA School, Birmingham

Nasir's First Riddle

What could it be?
Follow the clues and see.

It looks like **a monster**.
It sounds like **a roaring lion**.
It smells like **smoke**.
It feels like **a crocodile**.
It tastes like **sand**.

Have you guessed what it could be?
Look below and you will see,
It is...

Answer: A dragon.

Nasir (4)
Harper Bell SDA School, Birmingham

Esther's First Riddle

What could it be?
Follow the clues and see.

It looks like **a long snake**.
It sounds like **a big roar**.
It smells like **smoke**.
It feels **rough**.
It tastes like **a barbecue**.

Have you guessed what it could be?
Look below and you will see,
It is...

Answer: A dragon.

Esther Nealson (5)
Harper Bell SDA School, Birmingham

Ayanna's First Riddle

What could it be?
Follow the clues and see.

It looks like **a snake**.
It sounds like **a roar**.
It smells like **a fire**.
It feels like **a soft zebra**.
It tastes like **smoke**.

Have you guessed what it could be?
Look below and you will see,
It is...

Answer: A dragon.

Ayanna Mambrini (4)
Harper Bell SDA School, Birmingham

Tasia's First Riddle

What could it be?
Follow the clues and see.

It looks like **a snake**.
It sounds like **hissing**.
It smells like **fire**.
It feels like **sand**.
It tastes like **smoke**.

Have you guessed what it could be?
Look below and you will see,
It is...

Answer: A dragon.

Tasia Berryman (4)
Harper Bell SDA School, Birmingham

Isaac's First Riddle

What could it be?
Follow the clues and see.

It looks like **a circle**.
It sounds **gooey**.
It smells like **Granny's baking**.
It feels **squishy**.
It tastes like **chocolate**.

Have you guessed what it could be?
Look below and you will see,
It is...

Answer: A chocolate doughnut.

Isaac Richards (5)
Haughton St Giles Primary Academy, Haughton

Lily's First Riddle

What could it be?
Follow the clues and see.

It looks like **a cuddly toy**.
It sounds like **a cackle**.
It smells like **a unicorn**.
It feels **soft**.
It tastes like **strawberries**.

Have you guessed what it could be?
Look below and you will see,
It is...

Answer: Candyfloss.

Lily Duffett (5)
Haughton St Giles Primary Academy, Haughton

Amy's First Riddle

What could it be?
Follow the clues and see.

It looks like **a cloud**.
It sounds like **fun**.
It smells like **strawberry**.
It feels **sticky**.
It tastes like **sugar**.

Have you guessed what it could be?
Look below and you will see,
It is...

Answer: Candyfloss.

Amy Seville (5)
Haughton St Giles Primary Academy, Haughton

Axel's First Riddle

What could it be?
Follow the clues and see.

It looks like **a tower**.
It sounds like **animals**.
It smells like **poo**.
It feels **fluffy**.
It tastes like **sandwiches**.

Have you guessed what it could be?
Look below and you will see,
It is...

Answer: The zoo.

Axel Molinier (5)
Haughton St Giles Primary Academy, Haughton

Charlie's First Riddle

What could it be?
Follow the clues and see.

It looks like **a light with eight legs**.
It sounds like **bubbles**.
It smells like **the ocean**.
It feels **squishy**.
It tastes like **poison**.

Have you guessed what it could be?
Look below and you will see,
It is...

Answer: A **blue-ringed octopus**.

Charlie Elwell (4)
Highfields Primary School, Rowley Regis

Jennifer's First Riddle

What could it be?
Follow the clues and see.

It looks like **a horn, tail and cat paws**.
It sounds like **a miaow**.
It smells like **sweeties**.
It feels **squishy**.
It tastes like **sweeties**.

Have you guessed what it could be?
Look below and you will see,
It is...

Answer: A unicorn cat.

Jennifer Laura Floyd (4)
Highfields Primary School, Rowley Regis

Lola's First Riddle

What could it be?
Follow the clues and see.

It looks like **a bear**.
It sounds like **a car**.
It smells like **bamboo**.
It feels **warm**.
It tastes like **sweets**.

Have you guessed what it could be?
Look below and you will see,
It is…

Answer: A panda.

Lola Payton (4)
Highfields Primary School, Rowley Regis

Isabelle's First Riddle

What could it be?
Follow the clues and see.

It looks like **a fairy princess**.
It sounds like **a sunny summer's day**.
It smells like **my nanny**.
It feels like **a soft blanket**.
It tastes like **a horrible sandwich**.

Have you guessed what it could be?
Look below and you will see,
It is...

Answer: A rose.

Isabelle Davey (5)
Holywell Primary & Nursery School, Rubery

Jonah's First Riddle

Who could she be?
Follow the clues and see.

She looks like **a doll**.
She sounds like **a lion**.
She smells like **bath bubbles**.
She feels like **a warm hug**.
She tastes like **milk when we kiss her tummy**.

Have you guessed who she could be?
Look below and you will see,
She is…

Answer: **My baby sister, Zara.**

Jonah Clancy (5)
Holywell Primary & Nursery School, Rubery

Naomi's First Riddle

What could it be?
Follow the clues and see.

It looks like **fluffy clouds**.
It sounds like **soft feathers falling**.
It smells like **sweets and candies**.
It feels like **cotton wool melting**.
It tastes like **honey**.

Have you guessed what it could be?
Look below and you will see,
It is...

Answer: Candyfloss.

Naomi Gabriella Anne Young (5)
Holywell Primary & Nursery School, Rubery

Emilia's First Riddle

What could it be?
Follow the clues and see.

It looks like **squishy chocolate pud.**
It sounds like **a plank of wood.**
It smells like **the Earth.**
It feels like **crunchy dry sand.**
It tastes like **something very bland.**

Have you guessed what it could be?
Look below and you will see,
It is...

Answer: Mud.

Emilia Lynott (5)
Holywell Primary & Nursery School, Rubery

Piper's First Riddle

What could it be?
Follow the clues and see.

It looks like **a circle**.
It sounds **crunchy**.
It smells like **chocolate**.
It feels **bumpy and melty**.
It tastes **yummy**.

Have you guessed what it could be?
Look below and you will see,
It is...

Answer: A chocolate biscuit.

Piper Perkins (5)
Holywell Primary & Nursery School, Rubery

Lewis' First Riddle

What could it be?
Follow the clues and see.

It looks like **a cone**.
It sounds like ***slop, slop***.
It smells like **vanilla**.
It feels **cold**.
It tastes **sweet**.

Have you guessed what it could be?
Look below and you will see,
It is...

Answer: *Ice cream.*

Lewis Clarke (4)
Holywell Primary & Nursery School, Rubery

Gracie's First Riddle

What could it be?
Follow the clues and see.

It looks **brown and smooth**.
It smells like **sweeties**.
It feels **smooth and lumpy**.
It tastes **yummy**.

Have you guessed what it could be?
Look below and you will see,
It is...

Answer: Chocolate.

Gracie Medler (4)
Holywell Primary & Nursery School, Rubery

Noah's First Riddle

It lives in the sea.
It comes in all shapes and sizes.
It goes hunting when it's hungry.
People sing about it.
What is it?

Answer: *The baby shark song.*

Noah Holder (5)
Holywell Primary & Nursery School, Rubery

Evie's First Riddle

I am beautiful.
I am magical.
My body is white.
I have rainbow hair.
I have a long sharp horn.
What am I?

Answer: A unicorn.

Evie Clarke (4)
Holywell Primary & Nursery School, Rubery

Oliver's First Riddle

I am cold.
I am fluffy.
I am crunchy.
I am fun.
You can catch me on your tongue.
What am I?

Answer: Snow.

Oliver James Perry (4)
Holywell Primary & Nursery School, Rubery

Anneliese's First Riddle

What could it be?
Follow the clues and see.

It looks like **beach balls**.
It sounds like **seagulls**.
It smells like **the salty sea**.
It feels like **rough sand**.
It tastes like **sandwiches**.

Have you guessed what it could be?
Look below and you will see,
It is...

Answer: The beach.

Anneliese Cooper (4)
Martin Wilson School, Castlefields

Libby's First Riddle

What could it be?
Follow the clues and see.

It looks like **loud slides**.
It sounds like **noisy people**.
It smells like **cake**.
It feels like **children playing**.
It tastes like **cake**.

Have you guessed what it could be?
Look below and you will see,
It is...

Answer: *Little Rascals*.

Libby Hall (5)
Martin Wilson School, Castlefields

William's First Riddle

What could it be?
Follow the clues and see.

It looks like **chips with wings**.
It sounds **very loud**.
It smells **clean**.
It feels **cool and fast**.
It tastes like **cucumber sandwiches**.

Have you guessed what it could be?
Look below and you will see,
It is...

Answer: An aeroplane.

William Woolf-Farr (5)
Martin Wilson School, Castlefields

Ling's First Riddle

What could it be?
Follow the clues and see.

It looks like **leaves**.
It sounds like **robins**.
It smells like **rain**.
It feels like **wet puddles**.
It tastes like **hot chocolate**.

Have you guessed what it could be?
Look below and you will see,
It is...

Answer: *Forest School.*

Ling To (4)
Martin Wilson School, Castlefields

Florence's First Riddle

What could it be?
Follow the clues and see.

It looks **full of big toys**.
It sounds **noisy**.
It smells like **cake**.
It feels **hot**.
It tastes like **sandwiches**.

Have you guessed what it could be?
Look below and you will see,
It is...

Answer: *Little Rascals (play barn)*.

Florence Cheadle (5)
Martin Wilson School, Castlefields

Khaled's First Riddle

What could it be?
Follow the clues and see.

It looks like **a big land**.
It sounds like **a bee**.
It smells like **flowers**.
It feels like **snow**.
It tastes like **ice cream**.

Have you guessed what it could be?
Look below and you will see,
It is...

Answer: A park.

Khaled Al Mohammad (4)
Martin Wilson School, Castlefields

Maria's First Riddle

What could it be?
Follow the clues and see.

It looks **very big**.
It sounds like **children talking**.
It smells like **paper**.
It feels **hard**.
It tastes like **fish fingers**.

Have you guessed what it could be?
Look below and you will see,
It is...

Answer: *School.*

Maria Maunder (4)
Martin Wilson School, Castlefields

Bella-Rose's First Riddle

What could it be?
Follow the clues and see.

It looks like **slides**.
It sounds like **people**.
It smells like **flowers**.
It feels like **grass**.
It tastes like **sweets**.

Have you guessed what it could be?
Look below and you will see,
It is...

Answer: *The park.*

Bella-Rose Bowen (4)
Martin Wilson School, Castlefields

Sonny's First Riddle

What could it be?
Follow the clues and see.

It looks like **grass**.
It sounds like **dogs barking**.
It smells like **flowers**.
It feels **cold**.
It tastes like **crisps**.

Have you guessed what it could be?
Look below and you will see,
It is...

Answer: The park.

Sonny Ray Gibbons (5)
Martin Wilson School, Castlefields

Aiden's First Riddle

What could it be?
Follow the clues and see.

It looks **blue**.
It sounds like **seagulls**.
It smells like **chips**.
It feels **wet**.
It tastes like **ice cream**.

Have you guessed what it could be?
Look below and you will see,
It is...

Answer: *The beach.*

Aiden Morris (5)
Martin Wilson School, Castlefields

Layla's First Riddle

What could it be?
Follow the clues and see.

It looks like **water**.
It sounds like **splashing**.
It smells **clean**.
It feels **wet**.
It tastes **yuck**.

Have you guessed what it could be?
Look below and you will see,
It is...

Answer: A swimming pool.

Layla Haddock (5)
Martin Wilson School, Castlefields

Luna's First Riddle

What could it be?
Follow the clues and see.

It looks like **big rooms**.
It sounds **noisy**.
It smells like **fruit**.
It feels **safe**.
It tastes like **chips**.

Have you guessed what it could be?
Look below and you will see,
It is...

Answer: School.

Luna Morris (5)
Martin Wilson School, Castlefields

Indiana's First Riddle

What could it be?
Follow the clues and see.

It looks like **camouflage**.
It sounds like **a volcano erupting**.
It smells like **solid rock and pepper**.
It feels like **a fleecy jumper**.
It tastes like **vanilla and hot pepper**.

Have you guessed what it could be?
Look below and you will see,
It is...

Answer: *A tiger.*

Indiana Starr (4)
Moor Green Primary Academy, Moseley

Freya's First Riddle

What could it be?
Follow the clues and see.

It looks like **clear red glass**.
It sounds like **squelchy mud**.
It smells like **fresh strawberries**.
It feels like **wobbly slime**.
It tastes like **a yummy treat**.

Have you guessed what it could be?
Look below and you will see,
It is...

Answer: Strawberry Jelly.

Freya Lewis-Jackson (4)
Moor Green Primary Academy, Moseley

Laiba's First Riddle

What could it be?
Follow the clues and see.

It looks like **a circle**.
It sounds like **it's crunchy**.
It smells like **chocolate**.
It feels like **it's soft**.
It tastes like **it's sweet**.

Have you guessed what it could be?
Look below and you will see,
It is...

Answer: A chocolate cake.

Laiba Aslam (4)
Moor Green Primary Academy, Moseley

Zahra's First Riddle

What could it be?
Follow the clues and see.

It looks **round, square and triangular.**
It sounds like **bang, drop, beep.**
It smells like **ink.**
It feels like **wood and rubber.**
It tastes **bitter.**

Have you guessed what it could be?
Look below and you will see,
It is...

Answer: A stamp.

Zahra Assad Dar (4)
Moor Green Primary Academy, Moseley

Mabel's First Riddle

What could it be?
Follow the clues and see.

It looks like **a small tomato**.
It sounds like ***wibble, wobble***.
It smells like **sweets**.
It feels like **a cold jelly**.
It tastes like **mango**.

Have you guessed what it could be?
Look below and you will see,
It is...

Answer: *Ice cream.*

Mabel Orbach (5)
Moor Green Primary Academy, Moseley

Max's First Riddle

What could it be?
Follow the clues and see.

It looks like **a soft toy**.
It sounds like **woof, woof**.
It smells like **a wet blanket**.
It feels like **a cuddly toy**.
It tastes like **wet kisses**.

Have you guessed what it could be?
Look below and you will see,
It is…

Answer: A dog.

Max De Jong (4)
Moor Green Primary Academy, Moseley

Florence's First Riddle

What could it be?
Follow the clues and see.

It looks like **a statue**.
It sounds like **clip, clop, clip**.
It smells like **hay**.
It feels like **rough paper**.
It tastes like **a farmyard**.

Have you guessed what it could be?
Look below and you will see,
It is...

Answer: A pony.

Florence Orbach (5)
Moor Green Primary Academy, Moseley

Rory's First Riddle

What could it be?
Follow the clues and see.

It looks like **a stripy pony**.
It sounds like **a donkey**.
It smells like **fresh grass**.
It feels like **fur**.
It tastes like **sweets to a lion**.

Have you guessed what it could be?
Look below and you will see,
It is...

Answer: A zebra.

Rory Tyldesley Hosfield (5)
Moor Green Primary Academy, Moseley

Ava's First Riddle

What could it be?
Follow the clues and see.

It looks like **a wobbly pudding**.
It sounds like *slop*.
It smells like **sweets**.
It feels like **slime**.
It tastes like **strawberries**.

Have you guessed what it could be?
Look below and you will see,
It is...

Answer: Jelly.

Ava Roberts (5)
Moor Green Primary Academy, Moseley

Aria's First Riddle

What could it be?
Follow the clues and see.

It looks like **a rainbow**.
It sounds like **magical music**.
It smells like **fairy dust**.
It feels like **metal**.
It tastes like **glitter**.

Have you guessed what it could be?
Look below and you will see,
It is…

Answer: A magic wand.

Aria van Leeuwen (5)
Moor Green Primary Academy, Moseley

Finlay's First Riddle

What could it be?
Follow the clues and see.

It looks **brown and tasty**.
It sounds like *chomp*.
It smells **sweet and good**.
It feels **sticky**.
It tastes **delicious**.

Have you guessed what it could be?
Look below and you will see,
It is...

Answer: A chocolate cake.

Finlay Joe Biles (5)
Moor Green Primary Academy, Moseley

Amara's First Riddle

What could it be?
Follow the clues and see.

It looks like **a red ball**.
It sounds like **a crunch**.
It smells like **apple juice**.
It feels like **a hard ball**.
It tastes **very sweet**.

Have you guessed what it could be?
Look below and you will see,
It is...

Answer: An apple.

Amara Aisha Ali (4)
Moor Green Primary Academy, Moseley

Zahra's First Riddle

What could it be?
Follow the clues and see.

It looks like **a grasshopper**.
It sounds like **a shaker**.
It smells like **plastic**.
It feels like **a skinny snake**.
It tastes **yuck**.

Have you guessed what it could be?
Look below and you will see,
It is...

Answer: A Slinky. (upside down)

Zahra Hinds (5)
Moor Green Primary Academy, Moseley

Amelia's First Riddle

What could it be?
Follow the clues and see.

It looks like **ice**.
It sounds **so crunchy**.
It smells **really sweet**.
It feels like **snow**.
It tastes like **heaven**.

Have you guessed what it could be?
Look below and you will see,
It is...

Answer: A snow cone.

Amelia Suliman (4)
Moor Green Primary Academy, Moseley

Mariah's First Riddle

What could it be?
Follow the clues and see.

It looks like **a square**.
It sounds **chewy**.
It smells **sweet**.
It feels **squishy**.
It tastes like **a strawberry**.

Have you guessed what it could be?
Look below and you will see,
It is...

Answer: A Fruitella.

Mariah McEwan (4)
Moor Green Primary Academy, Moseley

Olivia's First Riddle

What could it be?
Follow the clues and see.

It looks **round and orange**.
It sounds **hollow**.
It smells like **a vegetable**.
It feels **hard and cold**.
It tastes like **butternut squash**.

Have you guessed what it could be?
Look below and you will see,
It is...

Answer: A pumpkin.

Olivia Potts (4)
Oswestry School, Oswestry

Florence's First Riddle

What could it be?
Follow the clues and see.

It looks **white and furry**.
It sounds like **a growl**.
It smells like **stinky socks**.
It feels **soft**.
It tastes like **fluff**.

Have you guessed what it could be?
Look below and you will see,
It is...

Answer: A polar bear.

Florence Everly Ruscoe (4)
Oswestry School, Oswestry

Edward's First Riddle

What could it be?
Follow the clues and see.

It looks like **a snake**.
It sounds like **sssss**.
It smells like **grass**.
It feels **bumpy**.
It tastes **yucky**.

Have you guessed what it could be?
Look below and you will see,
It is...

Answer: A lizard.

Edward Barker (4)
Oswestry School, Oswestry

Ella's First Riddle

What could it be?
Follow the clues and see.

It looks **round and yellow**.
It sounds **bumpy**.
It smells like **rubber**.
It feels **hairy**.
It tastes like **rubber**.

Have you guessed what it could be?
Look below and you will see,
It is...

Answer: A *tennis ball*.

Ella Osselton (4)
Oswestry School, Oswestry

Eleonora's First Riddle

What could it be?
Follow the clues and see.

It looks **fluffy**.
It sounds **squeaky**.
It smells like **woodland**.
It feels **furry**.
It tastes like **blood**.

Have you guessed what it could be?
Look below and you will see,
It is...

Answer: A rabbit.

Eleonora Rekikoski (5)
Oswestry School, Oswestry

Curran's First Riddle

What could it be?
Follow the clues and see.

It looks like **light paint**.
It sounds **crunchy**.
It smells **fresh**.
It feels **soft**.
It tastes **plain**.

Have you guessed what it could be?
Look below and you will see,
It is...

Answer: Snow.

Curran Dhawan (4)
Oswestry School, Oswestry

Roman's First Riddle

What could it be?
Follow the clues and see.

It looks like **a naughty black box.**
It sounds like **a whirly, beepy thing.**
It smells like **nothing, I checked.**
It feels like **a smooth, hard thing.**
Sometimes it gets warm.
It tastes like**... eurgh! Don't eat it!**

Have you guessed what it could be?
Look below and you will see,
It is...

Answer: A PlayStation.

Roman Lane (5)
Rugby Free Primary School, Rugby

Sophia's First Riddle

What could it be?
Follow the clues and see.

It looks like **a big, bald, green head**.
It sounds like **a hard balloon**.
It smells like **flowers**.
It feels like **a heavy football**.
It tastes like **a melting sweet sponge**.

Have you guessed what it could be?
Look below and you will see,
It is...

Answer: A watermelon.

Sophia Donnell (5)
Rugby Free Primary School, Rugby

Poppy's First Riddle

What could it be?
Follow the clues and see.

It looks like **a smile**.
It sounds like **squelchy mud**.
It smells like **medicine when I'm poorly**.
It feels like **a squidgy toy**.
It tastes like **my favourite milkshake**.

Have you guessed what it could be?
Look below and you will see,
It is...

Answer: A banana.

Poppy Wood (4)
Rugby Free Primary School, Rugby

Ruben's First Riddle

What could it be?
Follow the clues and see.

It looks like **a head**.
It sounds like ***pock-pock***.
It smells like **dirt, metal and firm branches**.
It feels **cold and ice cubey**.
It tastes like **crunchy steel**.

Have you guessed what it could be?
Look below and you will see,
It is...

Answer: A hammer.

Ruben Dijkstra (4)
Rugby Free Primary School, Rugby

Mia's First Riddle

What could it be?
Follow the clues and see.

It looks like **a man**.
It sounds like... **it doesn't speak**.
It smells like **ginger**.
It feels like **a soft biscuit**.
It tastes **sweet**.

Have you guessed what it could be?
Look below and you will see,
It is...

Answer: A gingerbread man.

Mia Lily Whittingham (4)
Rugby Free Primary School, Rugby

Anne's First Riddle

What could it be?
Follow the clues and see.

It looks like **it's fluffy**.
It sounds like **a squeak**.
It smells like **sawdust**.
It feels like **fluff**.
It tastes like **you don't eat it**.

Have you guessed what it could be?
Look below and you will see,
It is...

Answer: A hamster.

Anne Dewes (4)
Rugby Free Primary School, Rugby

Isaac's First Riddle

What could it be?
Follow the clues and see.

It looks like **a very long tree**.
It sounds like **a cow**.
It smells like **poo**.
It feels like **a snake**.
It tastes like **lunch for a T-rex**.

Have you guessed what it could be?
Look below and you will see,
It is...

Answer: A brachiosaurus.

Isaac Love (5)
Rugby Free Primary School, Rugby

Eliza's First Riddle

What could it be?
Follow the clues and see.

It looks like **a heart**.
It sounds **all swishy**.
It smells like **jam**.
It feels like **jelly**.
It tastes **all yummy in my tummy**.

Have you guessed what it could be?
Look below and you will see,
It is...

Answer: A nice red strawberry.

Eliza Houghton (4)
Rugby Free Primary School, Rugby

Theoren's First Riddle

What could it be?
Follow the clues and see.

It looks like **a pillow**.
It sounds like **silence**.
It smells like **sweets**.
It feels **squishy**.
It tastes like **milk**.

Have you guessed what it could be?
Look below and you will see,
It is...

Answer: A marshmallow man.

Theoren Wilson (4)
Rugby Free Primary School, Rugby

Teddy's First Riddle

What could it be?
Follow the clues and see.

It looks **wobbly**.
It sounds like *wibbly-wobbly*.
It smells like **strawberries**.
It feels **squidgy**.
It tastes **yummy**.

Have you guessed what it could be?
Look below and you will see,
It is...

Answer: Jelly.

Teddy James (4)
Rugby Free Primary School, Rugby

Khadeejah's First Riddle

What could it be?
Follow the clues and see.

It looks **feathery**.
It sounds like **pock, pock**.
It smells like **a roast**.
It feels **soft**.
It tastes **delicious**.

Have you guessed what it could be?
Look below and you will see,
It is...

Answer: A chicken.

Khadeejah Iftekhar (4)
Rugby Free Primary School, Rugby

Our First Riddle

What could it be?
Follow the clues and see.

It looks like **animals**.
It sounds like **oink!**
It smells like **smelly pigs**.
It feels **hairy**.
It tastes like **mud**.

Have you guessed what it could be?
Look below and you will see,
It is...

Answer: A farm.

Connor Wilshaw (5), Lillie Beckett (5) & Brooke
Squirrel Hayes First School, Biddulph

Our First Riddle

What could it be?
Follow the clues and see.

It looks **colourful**.
It sounds like **kids**.
It smells like **grass**.
It feels **soft**.
It tastes like **ice cream**.

Have you guessed what it could be?
Look below and you will see,
It is…

Answer: *The park.*

Maximus Hirst Malbon (5), Thomas & Shonalisa
Squirrel Hayes First School, Biddulph

Our First Riddle

What could it be?
Follow the clues and see.

It looks like **fish**.
It sounds like **splashing**.
It smells **yuck!**
It feels **wet**.
It tastes like **a picnic**.

Have you guessed what it could be?
Look below and you will see,
It is...

Answer: An aquarium.

Liam Rutter (5), Aiden Greensmith (5) & Oscar Till (5)
Squirrel Hayes First School, Biddulph

Our First Riddle

What could it be?
Follow the clues and see.

It looks like **two white balls**.
It sounds like *crunch, crunch*.
It smells like **fresh snow**.
It feels like **a cold ice cube**.
It tastes like **carrots and coal**.

Have you guessed what it could be?
Look below and you will see,
It is...

Answer: A snowman.

Ryan Rushid (5) & Sumayyah
St Anne's Catholic Primary School, Birmingham

Azeem's First Riddle

What could it be?
Follow the clues and see.

It looks like **a tall tree**.
It sounds like **humming**.
It smells like **something bad**.
It feels like **a teddy**.
It tastes like **something, I don't know what**.

Have you guessed what it could be?
Look below and you will see,
It is...

Answer: A giraffe.

Azeem Majid (5)
St Anne's Catholic Primary School, Birmingham

Eleesa's First Riddle

What could it be?
Follow the clues and see.

It looks **round and brown**.
It sounds like *grrr, growl*.
It smells like **sweet honey**.
It feels **soft and fluffy**.
It tastes **hairy**.

Have you guessed what it could be?
Look below and you will see,
It is...

Answer: A teddy bear.

Eleesa Manaa (5)
St Anne's Catholic Primary School, Birmingham

Alice's First Riddle

What could it be?
Follow the clues and see.

It looks like **cotton balls**.
It sounds like *pop, pop, pop*.
It smells like **butter**.
It feels **soft**.
It tastes **sweet or salted**.

Have you guessed what it could be?
Look below and you will see,
It is...

Answer: Popcorn.

Alice Boaretto Stuelp (4)
St Anne's Catholic Primary School, Birmingham

Michael's First Riddle

What could it be?
Follow the clues and see.

It looks like **a playground for sheep and pigs.**
It sounds **so noisy from the animals and tractor that digs.**
It **can be smelly because there is lots of poo.**
It feels **tickly when stroking the animals but the cow likes it. Moo.**
I bet it tastes **disgusting but I've never tried. Have you?**

Have you guessed what it could be?
Look below and you will see,
It is...

Answer: A farm.

Michael Gregory (5)
St Benedict's RC Primary Academy, Atherstone

Emily's First Riddle

What could I be?
Follow the clues and see.

I look like **I'm riding on a broom.**
I sound like **I'm going *zoom, zoom, zoom.***
I wear a pointy hat.
I have a black cat.
My spells look mucky and taste very yucky.

Have you guessed what I could be?
Look below and you will see,
I am...

Answer: *A witch.*

Emily Rose Owen (4)
St Benedict's RC Primary Academy, Atherstone

Henry's First Riddle

What could it be?
Follow the clues and see.

It looks **big and grey**.
It sounds like *snap* and *click* **when it closes its mouth**.
It smells like **the sea because that is where it lives**.
It feels **wet and slimy**.
It tastes like **fish because that's what it eats**.

Have you guessed what it could be?
Look below and you will see,
It is...

Answer: A shark.

Henry Scott (4)
St Benedict's RC Primary Academy, Atherstone

Jessica's First Riddle

What could it be?
Follow the clues and see.

Its body is **the shape of something it lays.**
It sounds **quiet so it can catch shrimps.**
It doesn't smell **but it has pink feathers.**
It feels like **standing on one leg.**
It has **a long neck and a beak to help grab its food.**

Have you guessed what it could be?
Look below and you will see,
It is...

Answer: A flamingo.

Jessica Scott (4)
St Benedict's RC Primary Academy, Atherstone

Sienna's First Riddle

My body is brown, lumpy and bumpy.
My hair is green, spiky and you can pull it out.
You have to take my skin off to make me yummy.
Sometimes I'm sweet and sometimes I'm savoury.
You can find me in a tin or on a plate.
I grow on a tree and fall to the ground.
I've even been known to be on your head.
My favourite thing to do is sunbathe.
What am I?

Answer: A pineapple.

Sienna Elsie Stone (4)
St Benedict's RC Primary Academy, Atherstone

Alexander's First Riddle

What could it be?
Follow the clues and see.

It looks **round, green and red inside with black seeds**.
It sounds **crunchy when you bite it**.
It smells **nice and sweet**.
It feels like **a hard, smooth ball**.
It tastes **sweet and very juicy**.

Have you guessed what it could be?
Look below and you will see,
It is...

Answer: A watermelon.

Alexander Theocharous (4)
St Benedict's RC Primary Academy, Atherstone

Natasha's First Riddle

What could it be?
Follow the clues and see.

It looks like **a fluffy ball**.
It sounds like **a squeaky toy**.
It smells like **hay**.
It feels like **a soft blanket**.
It tastes like... **you can't eat it**.

Have you guessed what it could be?
Look below and you will see,
It is...

Answer: A bunny.

Natasha Vanessa Radziwonka (4)
St Benedict's RC Primary Academy, Atherstone

Jeffrey's First Riddle

What could it be?
Follow the clues and see.

It looks like **two round balls**.
It sounds **crunchy**.
It smells like **happiness in the air**.
It feels like **freezing cold fluff**.
It tastes like **water**.

Have you guessed what it could be?
Look below and you will see,
It is...

Answer: A snowman.

Jeffrey Smith (5)
St Benedict's RC Primary Academy, Atherstone

Isabella's First Riddle

What could it be?
Follow the clues and see.

It looks like **a little flower**.
It sounds like **it's popping**.
It smells like **butter**.
It feels **crunchy and squidgy**.
It tastes **sweet or salty**.

Have you guessed what it could be?
Look below and you will see,
It is...

Answer: Popcorn.

Isabella Mobley (4)
St Benedict's RC Primary Academy, Atherstone

Milosz's First Riddle

What could it be?
Follow the clues and see.

It looks like **the blue sky**.
It sounds like **seashells**.
It smells like **a breeze**.
It feels like **water**.
It tastes like **salt**.

Have you guessed what it could be?
Look below and you will see,
It is...

Answer: *The ocean.*

Milosz Gaciag (5)
St Benedict's RC Primary Academy, Atherstone

Daisy's First Riddle

What could it be?
Follow the clues and see.

It looks **cold and furry**.
It sounds like **a bear**.
It smells like **fish**.
It feels **fuzzy and soft**.
It tastes like **fish**.

Have you guessed what it could be?
Look below and you will see,
It is...

Answer: A polar bear.

Daisy Taylor (5)
St Benedict's RC Primary Academy, Atherstone

Bobby's First Riddle

What could it be?
Follow the clues and see.

It looks like **a phone**.
It sounds like **slime**.
It smells like **a milkshake**.
It feels like **skin**.
It tastes **healthy**.

Have you guessed what it could be?
Look below and you will see,
It is...

Answer: A banana.

Bobby Hill (5)
St Benedict's RC Primary Academy, Atherstone

Apheia's First Riddle

What could it be?
Follow the clues and see.

It looks like **clouds**.
It sounds like *baa*.
It smells like **grass**.
It feels **soft**.
It tastes like **chops**.

Have you guessed what it could be?
Look below and you will see,
It is...

Answer: A lamb.

Apheia Thompson (5)
St Benedict's RC Primary Academy, Atherstone

Daniel's First Riddle

What could it be?
Follow the clues and see.

It looks like **a scary monster**.
It sounds like **a roaring tiger**.
It smells like **a bonfire**.
It feels like **a hot fire**.
It tastes like **crunchy bones**.

Have you guessed what it could be?
Look below and you will see,
It is...

Answer: A dragon.

Daniel George Machin (5)
St Thomas' CE (A) Primary School, Kidsgrove

Our First Riddle

What could it be?
Follow the clues and see.

It looks like **shiny stars**.
It sounds like **twinkling money**.
It smells like **rich people**.
It feels like **hard pebbles**.
It tastes like **chocolate coins**.

Have you guessed what it could be?
Look below and you will see,
It is...

Answer: *Money.*

Annabelle Massey (4) & Carter Smyk (5)
St Thomas' CE (A) Primary School, Kidsgrove

Our First Riddle

What could it be?
Follow the clues and see.

It looks like **pink sausages.**
It sounds like **a snuffly snort.**
It smells like **mud.**
It feels like **a smooth pancake.**
It tastes like **smoky bacon.**

Have you guessed what it could be?
Look below and you will see,
It is...

Answer: A pig.

William Dolman (5) & Lewis
St Thomas' CE (A) Primary School, Kidsgrove

Millie's First Riddle

What could it be?
Follow the clues and see.

It looks like **wiggly worms**.
It sounds **slurpy**.
It smells like **my yummy tea**.
It feels like **squishy snakes**.
It tastes like **spicy worms**.

Have you guessed what it could be?
Look below and you will see,
It is...

Answer: *Noodles.*

Millie Brown (4)
St Thomas' CE (A) Primary School, Kidsgrove

George's First Riddle

What could it be?
Follow the clues and see.

It looks like **pink jelly**.
It sounds like **it's snorting**.
It smells like **mud**.
It feels like **a soft jumper**.
It tastes like **sausages**.

Have you guessed what it could be?
Look below and you will see,
It is...

Answer: A pig.

George Halstead (4)
St Thomas' CE (A) Primary School, Kidsgrove

Esmae's First Riddle

What could it be?
Follow the clues and see.

It looks like **a trophy**.
It sounds like **jingle bells**.
It smells like **metal**.
It feels like **cold ice**.
It tastes like **a hard sweet**.

Have you guessed what it could be?
Look below and you will see,
It is...

Answer: *Gold coins.*

Esmae Murfitt (5)
St Thomas' CE (A) Primary School, Kidsgrove

Our First Riddle

What could it be?
Follow the clues and see.

It looks like **a rubbery snake**.
It sounds like **a roaring tiger**.
It smells like **smoke**.
It feels like **cold ice**.
It tastes like **fire**.

Have you guessed what it could be?
Look below and you will see,
It is...

Answer: A dragon.

Charlie Sambrooks (5) & Rhys Simcock (5)
St Thomas' CE (A) Primary School, Kidsgrove

Elliott's First Riddle

What could it be?
Follow the clues and see.

It looks like **a medal**.
It sounds like **glass smashing**.
It smells like **metal**.
It feels like **a trophy**.
It tastes like **hard rocks**.

Have you guessed what it could be?
Look below and you will see,
It is...

Answer: *Gold coins.*

Elliott Churchill (5)
St Thomas' CE (A) Primary School, Kidsgrove

Rowan's First Riddle

What could it be?
Follow the clues and see.

It looks like **a wiggly worm**.
It sounds like *roar!*
It smells like **burning**.
It feels like **spikes**.
It tastes like **fire**.

Have you guessed what it could be?
Look below and you will see,
It is...

Answer: A dragon.

Rowan Bennett (4)
St Thomas' CE (A) Primary School, Kidsgrove

Sammy's First Riddle

What could it be?
Follow the clues and see.

It looks like **a fish**.
It sounds like **roaring**.
It smells like **fire**.
It feels **fresh**.
It tastes like **bones**.

Have you guessed what it could be?
Look below and you will see,
It is...

Answer: A dragon.

Sammy Tunnicliffe (5)
St Thomas' CE (A) Primary School, Kidsgrove

Aimee's First Riddle

What could it be?
Follow the clues and see.

It looks like **gold**.
It sounds like **loud bangs**.
It smells like **chocolate**.
It feels like **tin foil**.
It tastes like **sweets**.

Have you guessed what it could be?
Look below and you will see,
It is...

Answer: *Coins.*

Aimee Rose Kathryn Phillips (4)
St Thomas' CE (A) Primary School, Kidsgrove

Kai's First Riddle

What could it be?
Follow the clues and see.

It looks like **spaghetti**.
It sounds like **a sloth**.
It smells like **fire**.
It feels like **worms**.
It tastes like **a takeaway**.

Have you guessed what it could be?
Look below and you will see,
It is...

Answer: Noodles.

Kai Murphy (5)
St Thomas' CE (A) Primary School, Kidsgrove

Layla's First Riddle

What could it be?
Follow the clues and see.

It looks like **a snake**.
It sounds like **a dinosaur**.
It smells like **smoke**.
It feels like **scales**.
It tastes like **fire**.

Have you guessed what it could be?
Look below and you will see,
It is...

Answer: A dragon.

Layla Beckensall (5)
St Thomas' CE (A) Primary School, Kidsgrove

Lexi's First Riddle

What could it be?
Follow the clues and see.

It looks like **gold**.
It sounds like **jingle bells**.
It smells like **perfume**.
It feels **cold**.
It tastes like **ice**.

Have you guessed what it could be?
Look below and you will see,
It is...

Answer: *Money*.

Lexi Rose Bloor (5)
St Thomas' CE (A) Primary School, Kidsgrove

Joshua's First Riddle

What could it be?
Follow the clues and see.

It looks **red**.
It sounds like **roaring**.
It smells like **smoke**.
It feels **hot**.
It tastes like **meat**.

Have you guessed what it could be?
Look below and you will see,
It is...

Answer: A dragon.

Joshua Dillion (4)
St Thomas' CE (A) Primary School, Kidsgrove

Jake's First Riddle

What could it be?
Follow the clues and see.

It looks **green with orange wings**.
It sounds like **roaring**.
It smells like **fire**.
It feels like **a spike**.
It tastes like **smoke**.

Have you guessed what it could be?
Look below and you will see,
It is...

Answer: *A dragon.*

Jake Sloane-Bulger (4)
Stoke Minster CE Primary Academy, Stoke-On-Trent

Victoria's First Riddle

What could it be?
Follow the clues and see.

It looks like **a square**.
It sounds like *crunch!*
It smells like **butter**.
It feels like **no crumbs**.
It tastes like **bread**.

Have you guessed what it could be?
Look below and you will see,
It is...

Answer: *Toast*.

Victoria Tivesi Gondwe (4)
Stoke Minster CE Primary Academy, Stoke-On-Trent

Dakota-Marie's First Riddle

What could it be?
Follow the clues and see.

It looks **white**.
It sounds like ***crunch!***
It smells like **fresh air**.
It feels **cold**.
It tastes like **icy water**.

Have you guessed what it could be?
Look below and you will see,
It is...

Answer: A snow scene.

Dakota-Marie Cole (5)
Stoke Minster CE Primary Academy, Stoke-On-Trent

Our First Riddle

What could it be?
Follow the clues and see.

It looks **brown**.
It sounds like *squelch!*
It smells like **chocolate**.
It feels **soft**.
It tastes **sweet**.

Have you guessed what it could be?
Look below and you will see,
It is...

Answer: A chocolate cake.

Erin Adams (5) & Skye
Stoke Minster CE Primary Academy, Stoke-On-Trent

Frankie's First Riddle

What could it be?
Follow the clues and see.

It looks **green**.
It sounds like **crunch!**
It smells like **fruit**.
It feels **furry**.
It tastes **sweet**.

Have you guessed what it could be?
Look below and you will see,
It is...

Answer: *A kiwi fruit.*

Frankie Bishop (4)
Stoke Minster CE Primary Academy, Stoke-On-Trent

Our First Riddle

What could it be?
Follow the clues and see.

It looks **yellow**.
It sounds like *crunch!*
It smells like **salt**.
It feels **hot**.
It tastes like **potato**.

Have you guessed what it could be?
Look below and you will see,
It is...

Answer: Chips.

Amadeus Wilson (4) & Jemimah
Stoke Minster CE Primary Academy, Stoke-On-Trent

Abdul's First Riddle

What could it be?
Follow the clues and see.

It looks **brown**.
It sounds like ***crunch!***
It smells **sweet**.
It feels **hard**.
It tastes like **sugar**.

Have you guessed what it could be?
Look below and you will see,
It is...

Answer: Chocolate.

Abdul Hannan (4)
Stoke Minster CE Primary Academy, Stoke-On-Trent

Hiba's First Riddle

What could it be?
Follow the clues and see.

It looks **big**.
It sounds like **horses**.
It smells like **food**.
It feels **cold**.
It tastes like **a king**.

Have you guessed what it could be?
Look below and you will see,
It is...

Answer: A castle.

Hiba Inayat (4)
Stoke Minster CE Primary Academy, Stoke-On-Trent

Aailyah's First Riddle

What could it be?
Follow the clues and see.

It looks **brown**.
It sounds **crunchy**.
It smells like **sugar**.
It feels **hard**.
It tastes **sweet**.

Have you guessed what it could be?
Look below and you will see,
It is...

Answer: *Chocolate.*

Aailyah Jefferies (5)
Stoke Minster CE Primary Academy, Stoke-On-Trent

Mohammad's First Riddle

What could it be?
Follow the clues and see.

It looks **yellow**.
It sounds **crunchy**.
It smells **nice**.
It feels **hot**.
It tastes like **salt**.

Have you guessed what it could be?
Look below and you will see,
It is...

Answer: Chips.

Mohammad Musa Tanveer (5)
Stoke Minster CE Primary Academy, Stoke-On-Trent

Isabella's First Riddle

What could it be?
Follow the clues and see.

It looks like **I'm holding an upside-down party hat.**
It sounds like **the words 'nice dream'.**
It smells like **a variety of flavours, but my favourite is mint.**
It feels like **squishy ice, but if I don't eat it quickly, it drips on my hand.**
It tastes like **a cold, sweet treat.**

Have you guessed what it could be?
Look below and you will see,
It is...

Answer: Ice cream.

Isabella Johanna Koch (5)
Stratford Preparatory School, Stratford-Upon-Avon

Florence's First Riddle

What could it be?
Follow the clues and see.

It looks like **two petals**.
It sounds like **whoosh, whoosh**.
It smells like **the wind**.
It feels like **silk**.
It tastes like... **you can't eat it**.

Have you guessed what it could be?
Look below and you will see,
It is...

Answer: A butterfly.

Florence Skelton (5)
Stratford Preparatory School, Stratford-Upon-Avon

Elizabeth's First Riddle

What could it be?
Follow the clues and see.

It looks **black and white**.
It sounds like **a police siren**.
It smells like **a flower**.
It feels like **silk**.
It tastes like... **I don't taste it**.

Have you guessed what it could be?
Look below and you will see,
It is...

Answer: A cat.

Elizabeth Robotham (5)
Stratford Preparatory School, Stratford-Upon-Avon

Alice-Rose's First Riddle

What could it be?
Follow the clues and see.

It looks like **a balloon on a stick**.
It sounds like **licking**.
It smells like **fruit**.
It feels **sticky**.
It tastes like **sweets**.

Have you guessed what it could be?
Look below and you will see,
It is...

Answer: A lollipop.

Alice-Rose Domoney (4)
Stratford Preparatory School, Stratford-Upon-Avon

Harriet's First Riddle

What could it be?
Follow the clues and see.

It looks like **snow**.
It sounds like **bells**.
It smells like **turkey**.
It feels **exciting**.
It tastes like **mince pies**.

Have you guessed what it could be?
Look below and you will see,
It is...

Answer: Christmas.

Harriet Griffiths (4)
Stratford Preparatory School, Stratford-Upon-Avon

Rory's First Riddle

What could it be?
Follow the clues and see.

It looks **fluffy**.
It sounds like **a growl**.
It smells **nice**.
It feels **soft**.

Have you guessed what it could be?
Look below and you will see,
It is...

Answer: A dog.

Rory Withers (4)
Stratford Preparatory School, Stratford-Upon-Avon

Levi's First Riddle

What could it be?
Follow the clues and see.

It looks like **it's tall and spotty**.
It sounds like **munch munch**.
It smells like **trees' leaves**.
It feels **smooth**.
It tastes like **an animal**.

Have you guessed what it could be?
Look below and you will see,
It is...

Answer: A giraffe.

Levi Dunn (5)
Timberley Academy, Birmingham

Poppy's First Riddle

What could it be?
Follow the clues and see.

It looks like **balls**.
It sounds like **a crack**.
It smells like **breakfast**.
It feels **slimy**.
It tastes like **it's been fried**.

Have you guessed what it could be?
Look below and you will see,
It is...

Answer: An egg.

Poppy Marie Nicholls (5)
Timberley Academy, Birmingham

Rayyan's First Riddle

What could it be?
Follow the clues and see.

It looks like **Lightning McQueen**.
It sounds like ***vroom, vroom***.
It smells like **oil**.
It feels like **smooth metal**.
It tastes like **dirt**.

Have you guessed what it could be?
Look below and you will see,
It is...

Answer: A car.

Rayyan Aiheve (4)
Timberley Academy, Birmingham

Ellie-Mai's First Riddle

What could it be?
Follow the clues and see.

It looks **white and black**.
It sounds like **baa**.
It smells like **an animal**.
It feels **soft and woolly**.
It tastes like **meat**.

Have you guessed what it could be?
Look below and you will see,
It is...

Answer: A sheep.

Ellie-Mai Draisey (4)
Timberley Academy, Birmingham

Jayden's First Riddle

What could it be?
Follow the clues and see.

It looks **red and round**.
It sounds like **crunch**.
It smells like **sweet juice**.
It feels like **a hard ball**.
It tastes like **green Starburst**.

Have you guessed what it could be?
Look below and you will see,
It is...

Answer: An apple.

Jayden Lees (5)
Timberley Academy, Birmingham

Carlisle's First Riddle

What could it be?
Follow the clues and see.

It looks **brown and feathery**.
It sounds like **tu-whit tu-whoo**.
It smells like **cotton candy**.
It feels **squashy**.
It tastes like **a bird**.

Have you guessed what it could be?
Look below and you will see,
It is...

Answer: *An owl.*

Carlisle Anatole (4)
Timberley Academy, Birmingham

Megan's First Riddle

What could it be?
Follow the clues and see.

It looks like **white rectangles**.
It sounds like **cracking**.
It smells like **milk**.
It feels **flat and cold**.
It tastes **crunchy**.

Have you guessed what it could be?
Look below and you will see,
It is...

Answer: Chocolate.

Megan Hennessy (4)
Timberley Academy, Birmingham

Rueben-Lee's First Riddle

What could it be?
Follow the clues and see.

It looks like **green sticks**.
It sounds like **crunch**.
It smells like **trees**.
It feels like **carpet**.
It tastes like **carrots**.

Have you guessed what it could be?
Look below and you will see,
It is...

Answer: *Grass*.

Rueben-Lee Pickett (4)
Timberley Academy, Birmingham

Hannah's First Riddle

Who could it be?
Follow the clues and see.

She looks like **sparkly scales**.
She sounds like **humming songs**.
She smells like **fish**.
She feels **wet**.
She tastes **lucky**.

Have you guessed who it could be?
Look below and you will see,
It is...

Answer: A mermaid.

Hannah Haji (4)
Timberley Academy, Birmingham

Kai's First Riddle

What could it be?
Follow the clues and see.

It looks like **a triangle**.
It sounds **crispy**.
It smells like **a tomato**.
It feels **hard**.
It tastes like **a crispy tomato**.

Have you guessed what it could be?
Look below and you will see,
It is...

Answer: A pizza.

Kai Teece (5)
Timberley Academy, Birmingham

Kaitlyn's First Riddle

What could it be?
Follow the clues and see.

It looks **big and scary**.
It sounds like *roar!*
It smells like **dirt**.
It feels **bumpy**.
It tastes like **mud**.

Have you guessed what it could be?
Look below and you will see,
It is...

Answer: A dinosaur.

Kaitlyn Collins (4)
Timberley Academy, Birmingham

Tommy's First Riddle

What could it be?
Follow the clues and see.

It looks like **a golden shape**.
It sounds **crunchy**.
It smells like **nuggets**.
It feels **hot**.
It tastes **yummy**.

Have you guessed what it could be?
Look below and you will see,
It is...

Answer: A chicken nugget.

Tommy Ray Hopton (5)
Timberley Academy, Birmingham

Joshua's First Riddle

What could it be?
Follow the clues and see.

It looks like **green and small**.
It sounds like **ribbet**.
It smells like **goo**.
It feels **wet**.
It tastes **not good**.

Have you guessed what it could be?
Look below and you will see,
It is...

Answer: A frog.

Joshua John Edwards (5)
Timberley Academy, Birmingham

Zachary's First Riddle

What could it be?
Follow the clues and see.

It looks like **yellow fire**.
It sounds like **pop**.
It smells like **hot flames**.
It feels **hot**.
It tastes **yucky**.

Have you guessed what it could be?
Look below and you will see,
It is...

Answer: The sun.

Zachary Sheldon (5)
Timberley Academy, Birmingham

Ray's First Riddle

What could it be?
Follow the clues and see.

It looks **soft and fluffy**.
It sounds **loud**.
It smells **normal**.
It feels **warm and soft**.
It tastes **meaty**.

Have you guessed what it could be?
Look below and you will see,
It is...

Answer: A cheetah.

Ray Jackson Maxwell (5)
Timberley Academy, Birmingham

Amarn's First Riddle

What could it be?
Follow the clues and see.

It looks like **cream**.
It sounds like **splashing**.
It smells like **fruit**.
It feels **cold**.
It tastes **nice**.

Have you guessed what it could be?
Look below and you will see,
It is...

Answer: A yoghurt.

Amarn Imran (4)
Timberley Academy, Birmingham

Maya's First Riddle

What could it be?
Follow the clues and see.

It looks **round**.
It sounds **squelchy**.
It smells like **orange juice**.
It feels **soft**.
It tastes **juicy**.

Have you guessed what it could be?
Look below and you will see,
It is...

Answer: An orange.

Maya Douglas (4)
Timberley Academy, Birmingham

Lexie-Louise's First Riddle

What could it be?
Follow the clues and see.

It looks **blue**.
It sounds like **whoosh**.
It smells like **the sky**.
It feels **cold**.
It tastes like **air**.

Have you guessed what it could be?
Look below and you will see,
It is...

Answer: *The wind.*

Lexie-Louise Rice (5)
Timberley Academy, Birmingham

Evan's First Riddle

What could they be?
Follow the clues and see.

They look **yellow**.
They sound **crunchy**.
They smell **yummy**.
They feel **crispy**.
They taste **salty**.

Have you guessed what they could be?
Look below and you will see,
They are...

Answer: Crisps.

Evan Ridsdill (5)
Timberley Academy, Birmingham

Vinnie's First Riddle

What could it be?
Follow the clues and see.

It looks like **a raindrop**.
It sounds **splashy**.
It smells **fruity**.
It feels **hard**.
It tastes **juicy**.

Have you guessed what it could be?
Look below and you will see,
It is...

Answer: A pear.

Vinnie Griffiths (4)
Timberley Academy, Birmingham

Casey-Rose's First Riddle

What could it be?
Follow the clues and see.

It looks like **the moon**.
It sounds **squelchy**.
It smells **fruity**.
It feels **soft**.
It tastes **soft**.

Have you guessed what it could be?
Look below and you will see,
It is...

Answer: A banana.

Casey-Rose Dutton-Jones (4)
Timberley Academy, Birmingham

Teah-Nevaeh's First Riddle

What could it be?
Follow the clues and see.

It looks **pink**.
It sounds **crunchy**.
It smells like **fish**.
It feels **squishy**.
It tastes like **fish**.

Have you guessed what it could be?
Look below and you will see,
It is...

Answer: A prawn.

Teah-Nevaeh Queely (5)
Timberley Academy, Birmingham

Violet's First Riddle

What could it be?
Follow the clues and see.

It looks **fluffy**.
It sounds like **woof, woof**.
It smells **furry**.
It feels **soft**.
It tastes like **fur**.

Have you guessed what it could be?
Look below and you will see,
It is...

Answer: A dog.

Violet Dunne (5)
Timberley Academy, Birmingham

Blake's First Riddle

What could it be?
Follow the clues and see.

It looks **green**.
It sounds **hard**.
It smells **nice**.
It feels **very hard**.
It tastes **really nice**.

Have you guessed what it could be?
Look below and you will see,
It is...

Answer: An apple.

Blake Powers (4)
Timberley Academy, Birmingham

Lewis' First Riddle

What could it be?
Follow the clues and see.

It looks **long**.
It sounds **crunchy**.
It smells **good**.
It feels **warm**.
It tastes **yummy**.

Have you guessed what it could be?
Look below and you will see,
It is...

Answer: Pasta.

Lewis Daniel Read (4)
Timberley Academy, Birmingham

Alicia's First Riddle

What could it be?
Follow the clues and see.

It looks like **it has a horn**.
It sounds like **a horse**.
It smells like **sweets**.
It feels **smooth**.

Have you guessed what it could be?
Look below and you will see,
It is...

Answer: A unicorn.

Alicia Rebecca McAdorey (4)
Timberley Academy, Birmingham

Lailah-Rose's First Riddle

What could it be?
Follow the clues and see.

It looks **soft**.
It sounds like **quack**.
It smells like **a pond**.
It feels **soft**.

Have you guessed what it could be?
Look below and you will see,
It is...

Answer: A duck.

Lailah-Rose Harris (4)
Timberley Academy, Birmingham

Isla's First Riddle

What could it be?
Follow the clues and see.

It looks **fluffy and white**.
It sounds like **baa**.
It smells **smelly**.
It feels **soft**.

Have you guessed what it could be?
Look below and you will see,
It is...

Answer: A sheep.

Isla Wilson (5)
Timberley Academy, Birmingham

Paisley's First Riddle

What could it be?
Follow the clues and see.

It looks like **all of the colours in the sky**.
It sounds like **a loud bang, *pop!***
It smells like **a smoky fire**.
It feels like **a cold night**.
It tastes like **sweet candyfloss**.

Have you guessed what it could be?
Look below and you will see,
It is...

Answer: *Bonfire Night.*

Paisley Rae Birks (5)
Weston Infant Academy, Weston Coyney

Our First Riddle

What could it be?
Follow the clues and see.

It looks like **twinkling lights**.
It sounds like **Santa's sleigh bells**.
It smells like **mince pie**.
It feels like **a warm cuddle**.
It tastes like **sprouts**.

Have you guessed what it could be?
Look below and you will see,
It is...

Answer: *Christmas.*

Rosie Reid (5), Jacob & Chloe Hilton (4)
Weston Infant Academy, Weston Coyney

Olivia's First Riddle

What could it be?
Follow the clues and see.

It looks like **a green colour**.
It sounds like **crunchy leaves**.
It smells like **the wind**.
It feels like **a smooth table**.
It tastes like **sandwiches**.

Have you guessed what it could be?
Look below and you will see,
It is...

Answer: It is the park!

Olivia Ritchie (4)
Weston Infant Academy, Weston Coyney

Our First Riddle

What could it be?
Follow the clues and see.

It looks like **twinkling lights**.
It sounds like **jingle bells**.
It smells like **mince pies**.
It feels like **cold snow**.
It tastes like **Christmas dinner**.

Have you guessed what it could be?
Look below and you will see,
It is...

Answer: *Christmas*.

Jack Edward Sidley (4), Millie-May Walklate (5), Caitlin Louise Sherratt (4) & Aayla
Weston Infant Academy, Weston Coyney

Rosalie's First Riddle

What could it be?
Follow the clues and see.

It looks **red**.
It smells like **sweets**.
It sounds like *snap*.
It tastes **good to eat**.

Have you guessed what it could be?
Look below and you will see,
It is...

Answer: An apple.

Rosalie Weston (5)
Weston Infant Academy, Weston Coyney

Our First Riddle

What could it be?
Follow the clues and see.

It looks like **little yellow clouds**.
It sounds like *crunch, crunch!*
It smells **yummy**.
It feels **round and lumpy**.
It tastes **sweet and salty**.

Have you guessed what it could be?
Look below and you will see,
It is...

Answer: Popcorn.

Evie Lawton (5) & Lana Williams (4)
Weston Infant Academy, Weston Coyney

Lacey's First Riddle

What could it be?
Follow the clues and see.

It looks like **a ball**.
It sounds like **it's full of juice**.
It smells like **sweets**.
It feels **bumpy**.
It tastes like **oranges**.

Have you guessed what it could be?
Look below and you will see,
It is...

Answer: An orange.

Lacey May Shaw (5)
Weston Infant Academy, Weston Coyney

Isabela's First Riddle

What could it be?
Follow the clues and see.

It looks **sparkly**.
It sounds like **crunchy leaves**.
It smells like **chocolate**.
It feels like **Christmas lights**.
It tastes like **chocolate**.

Have you guessed what it could be?
Look below and you will see,
It is...

Answer: Christmas.

Isabela Grace Davis (5)
Weston Infant Academy, Weston Coyney

Scarlett's First Riddle

What could it be?
Follow the clues and see.

It looks like **a red ball**.
It sounds like **a crunchy carrot**.
It smells like **sweets**.
It feels like **a banana**.
It tastes like **sweets**.

Have you guessed what it could be?
Look below and you will see,
It is…

Answer: An apple.

Scarlett Rose Kudlek (5)
Weston Infant Academy, Weston Coyney

Eliana's First Riddle

What could it be?
Follow the clues and see.

It looks like **colourful lights**.
It sounds like **chocolate**.
It smells like **pizza**.
It feels like **trees**.
It tastes like **pizza**.

Have you guessed what it could be?
Look below and you will see,
It is...

Answer: *Christmas.*

Eliana Sagoa (5)
Weston Infant Academy, Weston Coyney

Amelia-Grace's First Riddle

What could it be?
Follow the clues and see.

It looks like **lights**.
It sounds like **jingle bells**.
It smells like **mince pies**.
It feels like **an apple**.
It tastes like **pears**.

Have you guessed what it could be?
Look below and you will see,
It is...

Answer: A carrot.

Amelia-Grace Dunn (4)
Weston Infant Academy, Weston Coyney

Edward's First Riddle

What could it be?
Follow the clues and see.

It looks like **fun**.
It sounds like **noisy children**.
It smells like **toffee**.
It feels **cold**.
It tastes like **ham sandwiches**.

Have you guessed what it could be?
Look below and you will see,
It is...

Answer: The park.

Edward Leslie (5)
Weston Infant Academy, Weston Coyney

Freddie's First Riddle

What could it be?
Follow the clues and see.

It looks like **lights**.
It sounds like **smoke**.
It smells like **balloons**.
It feels like **apples**.
It tastes like **fire**.

Have you guessed what it could be?
Look below and you will see,
It is...

Answer: A firework.

Freddie Adamson (4)
Weston Infant Academy, Weston Coyney

Ruby-Jo's First Riddle

What could it be?
Follow the clues and see.

It looks like **a ball**.
It sounds like **squishy mud**.
It smells like **sweets**.
It feels **bumpy**.
It tastes like **sweets**.

Have you guessed what it could be?
Look below and you will see,
It is...

Answer: An orange.

Ruby-Jo Clewes (5)
Weston Infant Academy, Weston Coyney

Kacie-Jane's First Riddle

What could it be?
Follow the clues and see.

It looks like **a big tree**.
It sounds like **a carrot**.
It smells like **a baby wipe**.
It feels **smooth**.
It tastes **sweet**.

Have you guessed what it could be?
Look below and you will see,
It is...

Answer: *An apple.*

Kacie-Jane Slater (4)
Weston Infant Academy, Weston Coyney

Charlie's First Riddle

What could it be?
Follow the clues and see.

It looks **red and green.**
It sounds like **a carrot.**
It smells like **sweets.**
It feels **hard.**
It tastes like **orange.**

Have you guessed what it could be?
Look below and you will see,
It is...

Answer: An apple.

Charlie Milne (4)
Weston Infant Academy, Weston Coyney

Jesse's First Riddle

What could it be?
Follow the clues and see.

It looks like **a ball**.
It sounds like **a carrot**.
It smells like **a strawberry**.
It feels **hard**.
It tastes **sweet**.

Have you guessed what it could be?
Look below and you will see,
It is...

Answer: An apple.

Jesse James Fox (4)
Weston Infant Academy, Weston Coyney

Eva's First Riddle

What could it be?
Follow the clues and see.

It looks like **a ball**.
It sounds like **squishy mud**.
It smells like **sweets**.
It feels **bumpy**.
It tastes **juicy**.

Have you guessed what it could be?
Look below and you will see,
It is...

Answer: *An orange.*

Eva Barber (4)
Weston Infant Academy, Weston Coyney

Our First Riddle

What could it be?
Follow the clues and see.

It looks like **white balls**.
It sounds like *pop!*
It smells **sweet**.
It feels **crunchy**.
It tastes **sweet**.

Have you guessed what it could be?
Look below and you will see,
It is...

Answer: *Popcorn.*

George Pinto (5) & Eliza-Jayne
Weston Infant Academy, Weston Coyney

Sophie's First Riddle

What could it be?
Follow the clues and see.

It looks like **a ball**.
It sounds like **mud**.
It smells like **orange**.
It feels **soft**.
It tastes like **sweets**.

Have you guessed what it could be?
Look below and you will see,
It is...

Answer: An orange.

Sophie Rose Mundy (5)
Weston Infant Academy, Weston Coyney

Our First Riddle

What could it be?
Follow the clues and see.

It looks **yellow**.
It sounds **squishy**.
It smells like **sweets**.
It feels **soft**.
It tastes like **sweeties**.

Have you guessed what it could be?
Look below and you will see,
It is...

Answer: A banana.

Macie Banks (4), Jacob, Archie Mark Eastlake (4), Jack & Jaden
Weston Infant Academy, Weston Coyney

Our First Riddle

What could it be?
Follow the clues and see.

It looks **orange**.
It sounds **crunchy**.
It smells like **a garden**.
It feels **soft**.
It tastes **sweet**.

Have you guessed what it could be?
Look below and you will see,
It is...

Answer: A carrot.

Jacoby Blackaby (4) & Alesha Burley (4)
Weston Infant Academy, Weston Coyney

Guinevere's First Riddle

What could it be?
Follow the clues and see.

It looks **orange**.
It sounds **crunchy**.
It smells like **pepper**.
It feels **hard**.
It tastes **sweet**.

Have you guessed what it could be?
Look below and you will see,
It is…

Answer: A carrot.

Guinevere Bennett (4)
Weston Infant Academy, Weston Coyney

Lilly's First Riddle

What could it be?
Follow the clues and see.

It looks **orange**.
It sounds **crunchy**.
It smells like **plants**.
It feels **hard**.
It tastes **juicy**.

Have you guessed what it could be?
Look below and you will see,
It is...

Answer: A carrot.

Lilly Banks (4)
Weston Infant Academy, Weston Coyney

Harvey's First Riddle

What could it be?
Follow the clues and see.

It looks **yellow.**
It smells like **mud.**
It feels **squishy.**
It tastes like **grass.**

Have you guessed what it could be?
Look below and you will see,
It is…

Answer: A ball.

Harvey Mantle (4)
Weston Infant Academy, Weston Coyney

Cobie's First Riddle

What could it be?
Follow the clues and see.

It looks **red**.
It sounds **bouncy**.
It feels **cold**.
It tastes like **Christmas**.

Have you guessed what it could be?
Look below and you will see,
It is...

Answer: *Christmas.*

Cobie Thomas Emery (5)
Weston Infant Academy, Weston Coyney

Inaya's First Riddle

What could it be?
Follow the clues and see.

It looks like **a round, fat ball.**
It hears sounds **with sharp, pointy ears.**
It smells like **tree feathers.**
It feels like **a furry fluff ball.**
It tastes like **vomit.**

Have you guessed what it could be?
Look below and you will see,
It is...

Answer: An owl.

Inaya Choudhury-Rana (5)
Yardley Primary School, Birmingham

Noor-Alaynah's First Riddle

What could it be?
Follow the clues and see.

It looks like **red feathers**.
It sounds like *cluck, cluck*.
It smells like **fresh eggs**.
It feels **soft and coarse**.
It tastes like **chicken nuggets**.

Have you guessed what it could be?
Look below and you will see,
It is...

Answer: A hen.

Noor-Alaynah Usman (4)
Yardley Primary School, Birmingham

Xaavier's First Riddle

What could it be?
Follow the clues and see.

It looks **black and white**.
It sounds like ***moo, moo***.
It smells like **white milk**.
It feels **soft and smooth**.
It tastes like **a cheeseburger**.

Have you guessed what it could be?
Look below and you will see,
It is…

Answer: A cow.

Xaavier Mahmood (4)
Yardley Primary School, Birmingham

Joel's First Riddle

What could it be?
Follow the clues and see.

It looks **big and grey**.
It sounds like **a fish**.
It smells like **a pongy fish**.
It feels like **a slippery tongue**.
It tastes like **awful fish**.

Have you guessed what it could be?
Look below and you will see,
It is...

Answer: A whale.

Joel Mason (5)
Yardley Primary School, Birmingham

YOUNG WRITERS INFORMATION

We hope you have enjoyed reading this book – and that you will continue to in the coming years.

If you're a young writer who enjoys reading and creative writing, or the parent of an enthusiastic poet or story writer, do visit our website www.youngwriters.co.uk. Here you will find free competitions, workshops and games, as well as recommended reads, a poetry glossary and our blog. There's lots to keep budding writers motivated to write!

If you would like to order further copies of this book, or any of our other titles, then please give us a call or order via your online account.

Young Writers
Remus House
Coltsfoot Drive
Peterborough
PE2 9BF
(01733) 890066
info@youngwriters.co.uk

Join in the conversation!
Tips, news, giveaways and much more!